Poetry from My Heart

I0117213

LM Scatizzi

chipmunkapublishing
the mental health publisher

Published by
Chipmunkapublishing
PO Box 6872
Brentwood
Essex CM13 1ZT
United Kingdom

http://www.chipmunkapublishing.com

Chipmunkapublishing gratefully acknowledge the support of Arts Council England.

Author Biography

Lucy Scatizzi was born in 1961 in Trieste, Italy & was diagnosed schizophrenic in 1984. After several major breakdowns she has settled into a quiet life in the last decade.

She is vegetarian and her interests include pacifism, nature and ecology, music (particularly the guitar), Buddhism, aid work, and literature and art. She enjoys walks in natural surroundings.

She hopes this book will be inspirational for life and world changing good deeds, thoughts and actions.

LM Scatizzi

Part 1

KIDS LIKE MOTHS

IMPRESSIONS

A fertile plain, wheat fields
Each ear of corn dear to its creator
Beautiful, feathery & rich –
A promise for a good year.
But Mr. D. did not think of this
As he rode towards town on
The morning train.
In his suit & tie he barely glanced from
His newspaper
Where stocks & bonds proved
More indicative of what mattered to him.
The fields were but a blur outside the dust smeared window
A plain of profit, not of food.

WHY

Foam flecked the little foal sees the light
And from the moment it gains its sight
It is provided for.
Grass & a fur coat –
Freedom & life one thing.
I don't understand
Why can't we live off the land
Instead of going batty like lords
In a race for credits, mortgages & words?

KIDS LIKE MOTHS

Fling themselves at the light bulb
In varying degrees of desperation
Get burned
The scorched wings leave hates
To be worked out at a later date
Into bits of wisdom.

THE FOOL ON THE HILL

Infinitely wise
Is the guy in disguise
Who sits on the hill
With his sunglasses on
Waiting for the sun to set
Wearing his heart on his sleeve.

Smattering of sunshine on my pillow
I write to capture its rays
As if tomorrow it may stop shining.

FEELINGS OF A BACK COUNTRY JERKIN

Here I hang on the wall
Workin' day done
My sleeves still bent at the elbow
Watching my owner
Muse upon the meaning of life.
The light is dim
The night upon us
A moth flutters around the lamp
And my owner is alone.
I know him, alone he walks
Through the days
Alone he stands
In the pub at night.
We jackets have an understanding
Like the dogs & chicks & panda bears
Unlike these humans
Who work over the limits
Of their own understanding
And against their own interests.
DIED PEACEFULLY IN THEIR SLEEP

They lay awake
To sleep to slake
The thirst for love
For things above
To wonder
About the future beyond the thunder
Of their warm hearts.
They wanted to be smart
And really go deep
Die peacefully in their sleep.

GRACELAND

There was an aficionado
Of the American way of life
Wrote songs about it
Charmed me into the night.
There was an African beat to his stories
Guitar, chimes & penny whistles
And though he's an intellectual
I think he's outta sight.

THE LIZARD

I BAKE ON THIS STONE
Happy alone
With no sense of dread
I can sense you all
Some a light tread
Some a heavy squall
Dew drops & sun
Are my sense of fun
No sins I have to atone.

Poetry from My Heart

RESPECT

I'D LIKE TO BE A GOOD WORKING MACHINE
But not so much
That I'd sell my soul
For a bowl
Of your bitter contempt.

Hey Flynn, fling us a spanner
Got to fix this
'Cos this thing is civilization.

Is not beautiful
Is cute
Beats on regardless
This old heart of mine.

DRAUGHT HORSE

A draught horse clanking along the track
Clop trot clop trot clop trot
The dust & rain slip off the slanting hooves
Clop trot clop trot clop trot
The harness shines brown, dull gold & black
Clop trot clop trot clop trot
The appledy eyes' tired leisurely sheen
Clop hop.

MUTUAL LOVE

It's hard to find
Love is trust
Sharing the last crust
With someone who removes the rust
And clears your mind.

SOLILOQUY

Is it fate
Is it the body
Is it the mind
Is it love?
One life to live
One joke to share
Ultimately it's you
Jumping around
Live.
LIFE'S LIKE THAT

With this young lamb I romp
Me a child of seven
I pull its fur
I tug its neck
And it understands my play.
At school I worry over my books
To learn to read & write & say
What is intelligent, I pray.
Then at dinner I will eat
My friend the lamb's so tender be
And think of Jesus & a question be
If he came back would he be on tv?

THE MOON

Circle of beauty
Lover's light
Lets its unblushing face
Grow & fade & grow again
In nature's innocence.

CROCUS

A long nose
Between the tulips
She toys with him
He chases her
Old people.

THE BEAST

The mad beast
Bloodthirsty
Cruel
Roams about at the icy midnight hour
Dragging in its wake
The three-legged limp
Of a doe-like creature.

TO THE ETHIOPIAN KIDS

You don't wonder about philosophy
You live it
Having no rights you have more
And may the depth of your existence
Not lose its sweetness as it loses its pain.

TEARS, LOVE & FRUSTRATION

On the shores of some distant land
Like today we know no more
All hopes live
They are not so far off & remote
That they will not
Fulfilled
Visit us from time to time,
There are those still however
Which hide in the furthest reaches of that country
And are fed with salty tears
                              love

& frustration.

THE GUN

Smooth & shiny is my holster
New and glistening like glycerine
Close up you can see the network
Of the leather's cells
In it I keep
A bunch of keys
And should you try to harm me
I'd lock you up.

SHUSH

I am ignorant, I know
There's so much you have to show
Don't take advantage
Of my inability
I won't be a liability.

THE WAR PLANE

It circles
Closer & closer
And settles
On a dollar note.

A POET

A poet sat under a brambly bush
Composed a sonnet
For the wee sunny rabbit
He had set a snare for
With rumbly tummy.

He stoked the fire
Wiped his hands of the mire
And when he saw his supper approaching
Jumped up to scare him away.

SOMEDAY

Someday the sun is going to shine
On rusty guns
& overgrown
Adding machines.

RAIN WITHOUT CLOUDS

In the salad (nicoise) of my thoughts
The sun is always shining sometime
And the stars are always bright
'Cos that's the truth.
And when I talk (like a lunatic)
Laugh or cry
Or think or try
To find some new expression
Me is somewhere inside
Sleeping & guarded
Thinking though there be miles
Between outside & inside
Life is sweet
Like rain without clouds.

SPARK

There is so much to what you are
It never ends
You try & guess the dark parts
Clean them up
Banish them
Then you're left with grey thoughts
Whisping into your consciousness
And when you've stopped feeling them
There's the white brilliance
Of a funny spark of happiness.

WHAT THE HELL?

What kind of world is this
Where you have to pay to live?

GIVE IT TIME

When the tears have not yet dried
Give it time
When the tears have to be cried
Give it time
When the soul is not satisfied
Give it time
When your love has been badly tried
Give it time
In the end it will all have been
Worth someone's while
So smile.

THE LOCH NESS MONSTER IS PATHETIC

Why does she fix with persistent stare
The spot where I would want to come up for air
For I wish not to be seen & lose my credibility
I am Nessie famed for invisibility
So until she returns to read her book
To deeper waters I must be took
Oh welcome the night
When no one can be sure of his sight
When I come up to give them a fright.

HUMPHREY LOVE

It's all right
Rest your weary eyes on my shoulder
Rest your soppy heart on my jumper
It's all right
Leave your shattered dreams
On my nape
Cry a few tears to clear your eyes
And it's all right.

DON'T LET LOVE PASS YOU BY!

Love as sweet as the gentlest touch
Of a little hand asking for a hug
Love as wild & blue
As a dream just out of touch
Love as warm & laughing
As your lover saying your name
Once again
Love as green & luscious
As the world bearing the weight
Of a whole creation
And carefully feeding it
Love crippled & shackled
In the hearts of the broken
And through plasters or twisted
Still fighting on
Love lucid & tender
In freedom's defender
A smile on his face
As he fixes his eye
On man's higher nature.

FIGHT FOR PEACE

Torture the torturers by not giving in
Bleed their stony hearts from within
Haunt their mansions & houses
With the smiling laughter
Of those they would have taken
Stake out banners of freedom
On washing lines and the tall, gaunt flagpoles
Of your nations
Keep the dead alive
And smile a mocking smile
For peace called for
With gun in hand.

THE FUTURE THAT CAME & WENT

On the meadows we sat
Sun going down on the flat
The children were playing
All colours and saying:
When we grow up.

That day in the future
Never mind all the nature
We men have the power
When we grow up.

That day finally came
But things weren't the same
The power was voracious
The flat was built up.

On the doorsteps we sat
Sun going down on the flat
The children's children were playing
All colours & saying
When we grow up.

WILL?

Will that day ever come
When we will sort of be one
And know that sweetish secret
You've got everything coming
If what you're asking ain't much.

THE MOGGY MONSTER

The moggy monster
Sits curled into a bubble
Laughing in his belly
He knows the truth
And s'truth
It is funny.

ELF-LIKE PEOPLE

Elf-like people
Build elaborate systems
Flowers of creation
But then
Who believes in elves?

FAITHFUL

I sit by the sea
Water running over my toes
And think of you
I think long
I think hard
And come up with the same answer
You.

HARD ROCK BLUE

The knight errant
Of his own desires
Has faith that is lost
Even to himself
So he fights on
In the hope
That truth will win the day.

THE GRIM REAPER

Death the reaper
Grim & stark
Faceless outline
Scathing sickle
Not to be laughed at
Not to be feared
Leaves no imprint
On your soul.

SAPLINGS

Three foot, four foot, five foot
Young & pliant
Strong & sturdy
Mop-haired imps
Bending supple
To & fro from school.

THE COOL DUDE

Whatever you think
He does it better
But he don't show it
Oh no
He bats his eyelashes
And pulls his woolly scarf
One notch tighter.

THE ECONOMY

The economy
Is a web of ignominy
The fantasy of a stockbroker
His substitute for a game of poker
The many natural resources
Backed like so many race horses
Put under sedation
And there we have inflation
Is there nothing to this game
Besides the pursuit of gain?

WAR

The ultimate idiocy
Of a scavenging few
Followed by millions
Who all pay their due

INHERITANCE

A fragmented bog of superstitions
Stemming from the fear of death
A world natural & ever-renewing
A wealth of knowledge to be discovered
Infinite possibility of freedom
Together with sense & responsibility
All to be understood.

SUNSHINE IN THE AUTUMN

Shadows play upon the wall
And in the net of dancing leaves
A tear drop runs unnoticed
And cutting up against the sun
You bend down to console me
And over in the tree
A squirrel chasing nuts
Whisps across the sun's face.

YOSEMITE VALLEY

Down I go
To Yosemite Valley
To get some food
To bring to you
You look at me
Say nothing
And my sweat dries on my skin.

STONED WASH-HOUSE BLUES

Got an earful of shampoo
Under suds the water's blue
Took a skid out to the soap
Climbed back out by a piece of rope
Splashed about till my hair was wet
The amount of dirt was worth a bet
Cleaned my knees my ears my nose
Yea the luxury of a garden hose
It's the practice of a bath
In the country of bluegrass.

THE CAULDRON

Simmering on a bubbly flame
The cauldron of emotions
Distilled slowly with perfume
The essence of reason
Made tangy with a smile
The hectic ponderings of pain
Sipping sweet longings slowly
We stew restlessly
In a sea of conflicting information.

SORROW

I have been everywhere
I am going nowhere
My soul has been shattered across the land
Great splinters of ice have taken over my soul
Standing erect it crouches
Against another whiplash wind of reality
Or is it reality?

FRIENDSHIP

I told you the moon was out of reach
That's why I liked looking at it
You told me
Your life was an endless search
That's why you liked getting somewhere
I skimmed stones over to the bridge
You sifted pebbles through your hands
And we watched the ducks preen.

GOING PLACES

Jet-setters
Trend-setters
Millionaires
Have you made it
To where I'm going
Miners
Joiners
Farmers
Have you paved the road
Teachers
Preachers
Scientists
Have you planted
Signposts on the verge?
I'll make it on foot,
I don't need a hearse.

SPRING

Rosy sunlight bathing over
Lemon green grass & primroses
A big pumpkin sun awaits in the summer
But now the butterflies see dawn
Bamboo shoots nuzzle the pale blue thin air
Spring of another tremulous year
Clean colours, clean smells
Bashful alliance with nature
Thinks the peaceful bear emerging.

WHO SAYS?

The man says
The future looks violent
Only the smart will get wise
Streetwise
Who says?
The card says
The future is money
Flexibility is the key
To a heart
Who says
The masses & millions
The counted statistics
The gleaming ballistics
Who says?

SHARK

Hulk
Awesome rubbish eater
Primitive lad of the deep
No compulsion
But to be mindless
When not engaged
In some lighter activity.

REBEL

I'm not going to let you
Ruin our world
I'm not going to stop you, that's all.
You'll see sense.

ECOLOGICAL THOUGHT

Keep in mind
All the tomorrows
As you take a good look
At today.

NATURAL HIGH

Well look at it all
And though I be small
There's some things that make you feel
10 feet tall.

SOME MOODS

Are inconclusive
The solution remains
Elusive.

THE FIRING SQUAD

Silence
The sound of a shot
A young life
Is on this spot.

(In memory of South American urchins).

FLUFF

I am an island, even if no man is
And to build up resources
Against all kinds of discourses
And be an individual
Is my main policy.
The central government
Of my dippy island
Is for the heavens to invent
And the revenue is small
But by all means sufficient.

SCOWL

I disagree
I don't see why
You so stubbornly deny
What I would have you
Believe in.
(Sigh)

ESSENTIALLY ALIVE

The scarecrow said
I'd rather give my life
Than hold a job from nine till five
Midnight to midnight
Is more essential to me
For a scarecrow I am and a scarecrow I be.

TENDER

Yearning, like smooth skin
To see what's best for you
Happen.

NO HELL

There is no hell
No man, no hell
But the one you made
And even that will fade.

WHY NO SANCTIONS?

Show me a dead man
And I'll show you a saint
Show me a dead man
And I'll show you a quaint
Saying that goes
Thou shalt not kill
Show me a soldier
That fits the bill.

BOOGEY MAN

When your problems get too heavy
Share them with the boogey man
He'll say come on savvy
Plenty more where they came from
Look at the other side of th'levy
Find yourself something to smile upon.

MAD DOG

Mad dog
Rabid rabid
Roams the city streets
Mad dog
Rabid rabid
Is going to get you someday
Politician's candour
Disguises his rapid sway
Politician's candour
Opens up the door
When mad dog rabid rabid
Is going to have his way.

(Rolling Stones concert 1990)

IRAQ & SO ON

Peace hides its sleepy head
Behind mountains of obstinacy
While dogma rushes in
And takes up the flag.
And drops it!

AGE

Am as old as the hills
As young as a fawn
Am as weary as an old soldier
As fresh as blueberry juice
As tired as a clock
As rested as a stream
I will wait
For another day.

MORNING POST

Buried under a pile of bills
I smile like a crab
Trying to find his way
From under a carcass.

LISTENING TO BOB DYLAN DURING THE GULF WAR

The ancient spirits gather
Around the witches' brew
The slick is almost brittle
And everything is new.
There is a sense in nonsense
Exclaims the wicked bard
He is not as bad as he seems
So he sure comes down hard.
The war drums roll in rising hum
As the flinty witches whicker
They stir the blood
And the fog is getting thicker.
The bard he sings
About the things
The soldier missed as he dies at twenty.
The loves, the waits, the lives and fates
Killed by the oldest war,
Made by the men with plenty.

THE SIMPLETON

I see
And understand
More than you would think
From the way I look
My friend.
And often I muse
Is the world out of kilter
Or is it just I
Who am out of touch?

MOTORCYCLE MAD

Hop Jump Run Yeo
Molded metal grasshopper
Laughing clear into the sun
Running away from duties
No one should need to perform
Duty-free whiz.

THE MACHINE (CORN CHIPS)

The machine turns out twisted effluvium
Of opulence
Cogs turn shining to a new day
The frankincense & MYRRH OF MONEY TALKS
Brought with gold to the altar of progress
In a giant misapprehension of the urgency of life
In the back streets & alleys
Of the natives of this land
The power of unfettered thought
Not given precedence
Over the power of electric computing of minutes
Sufficiency & love remain an elusive dream
The governments fail to pursue?

HORIZONS

Let the mind roam
On the paths of the nearly known
A world of promise
A world sometimes to recoil from
And bounce back, resilient
To see the beauty
And know the peace.

SUNSET

An old lady alone
Peeling potatoes or shelling peas
Sitting on her front porch
Watching the sunset
Behind a half moon of pines
She has seen many children grow
Though not necessarily all her own
And as she sifts the peas and gathers the potato peels
She prays for the world to be better.

EVERYDAY OCCURANCES (MONETARISM)

The motion of a train
The drawing of a bucket from a well
The sound of someone sleeping
The emission of a radio
The creak of the jungle being felled
The vegetation growing
Another car passing by
The silence of the stones
And the everlasting exchange of money.

MEMORY OF THE FIRST MOON LANDING

Swiss cheese turned to apple crumble
In the craters of the moon
Powdery puffs of the moon's fine dust
Fluffing up the camera's lens
As the first steps of the deep sea divers
Of the sky before my still
Big eyes of the under eight
Sunk in a sofa in wakeful sleep
In the deep of the moonlit night
Only now the moon doesn't shine
In the sky but from a TV screen
While a commentator excitedly
Reports: "One small step for man"
One giant leap for mankind."

LONG RANGE IMPLICATIONS

Eternity was written all over it
The green & blue and brown globe with its sheath of
clouds
Eternity was sung by the prophets
And questioningly invoked by the dying
Yet no long range plans were made for it
By the people grouped in anthill-like cities
And scattered like rain along the countryside
Nothing but token intentions, with the clue unsolved
The rain forests dying, the waters poisoned
The rain falling acid, and the air chokes
And still the humans toil on, to build more furnaces
More gadgets, more cars, to amuse themselves
While their souls strive towards the rest of eternity
And fail to grasp it?

LEGEND

Feathers for hair
A dewdrop of a nose
Two perplexed and numb eyes
Startled by the sudden rush of light
That was you
In your first moments
The spark of life you gave yourself
Grew with the challenges
That faced you
Until old and with skin like parchment paper
You laid your bony head down
And your life history
Remains just a legend
On a south facing stone.

JEWEL (A DOT IN THE GALAXIES)

Howling at the stars
In desperation
In sheer frustration
Why is the world
Not as I would have it
A perfect jewel
With everybody happy?

NO ONE (BLINDNESS)

Why ever that
What ever for
How can it be
Who is so sure
That they can answer
What needs must be
And what is not
And we cannot see.

SMOKESTACK LIGHTNING

Ride on your steed of thoughts
I don't ride on the same horse
As you all of the time
But we share the same mounts
And I'm going to the same place
The cemetery of oppression
The graveyard of greed
The birthplace of laughter
The wind a soft caress.

FACE

I trace your eyes
Your lashes tickle me
Down your nose I glide
To the dry dampness of your lips
Under your chin I stop
Retrace my steps
Up to the sandy feeling of your brows
I love your hair
It fills my hands like silk
Your head is merely bulk
For your smile.

LM Scatizzi

Part 2

SELF THE HORSE

ALL THAT MONEY CAN BUY

I've got a tree to give me shade
Whatever my mood be
It is the tree made from the wood
Of all the lavatory paper I have used
So too a river of electricity
A mountain of food
An atmosphere of air
A lake of petrol and so on
This landscape ought to make me grateful
But it just makes me despondent.

BITE IT

Milk will flow
The money grows on trees
Clouds rain coca cola
(That's a new one)
Mangoes are good for juggling
And there are many ways
To fuel your legs
Time runs back and forth
The split atom is perhaps a mishap
And the magnitude of our consumption
Reforms itself in various shapes.

BITTER SWEET LIFE

Tho' I have all I need
Others do not
So I lack too
Tho' I want nothing
Others do
Thus the ground shifts
Western culture
The worship of the ephemeral.

BLUE GRASS

I rode on whatever transport was at hand
Out into the wide blue yonder
Left my home town far behind
Slept beneath the stars and the tightening of thunder

Met people of all descriptions
But no one came close to me as you
Dear musician of the dark blue skies
You guided me as I came through

Came back home a suntan richer
And a longing for simple things
Couldn't fathom society's many trappings
Guess I got myself a pair of wings.

BRITAIN

Limestone caves
Midnight raves
Overworked pubs
Dole cheque subs
Hopes and dreams
Written pages by the reams
These British Isles
Islands to be reckoned with
Islands to be done with
And come back.

CENTRE OF THE WORLD

Contrary to the belief of many
The centre of the world
Is in the middle of the earth
Not your self.

CLOCKS AND WATCHES

Hours that glide by
Placidly serene
Fragmented by activity
Or with explosions of emotion
Hours that linger in the mind
When colours are experienced vividly
Fraternal bonds are made
And something unexplained becomes clear
Hours spent in making plans
Petty trivial plans
And schemes of inordinate newness
Hours lost in the recesses of memory
Concealed behind the present time
Hours that make up our lives.

COMMON DREAMS

This is your dream
This is my dream
We dream together
Is that reality?

COPING WITH AFFLICTION

Let your spirits fly on a paper plane
Play football with your ball and chain
Swing from your crutches
Dance with your Zimmer frames
Race with your wheelchairs
Let your madness be reason
Listen with blind eyes
Watch with deaf ears
Sing a song with a novel accent
Leave sorrow behind
Find the happiness of normality
Closeted within your originality.

COURAGE IN THE SUN (on the road)

The road was long and without shade
It shone in the far distance
The glare of the sun on the tarmac
Made my head ache
My future looked like the end of the road
Always out of reach
Then I had a glass of water
Cool, life-line quick, refreshing
And decided my future was here
Under the glare of the sun
Though there was no shade
My courage was a lot of fun.

CROCK 'O SHIT

Walking alone
Along the debris of an old city
Which is still alive
Thinking what a nightmare
This civilization is.
(Only sometimes 'tho).

DEATH HEAD MOTH

The young moth, a preacher
On the point of mega annoyance
Said to his wishful soul mate
Something slightly obscene,
A crane fly flew by outside.
He'd been slammed by me, accidentally
For sitting in the wrong spot
(I reached for my money box).
I will rescue you from misery I said
Giving him a tissue to eat, the day previously
He revived and disappeared
(Or perhaps, whatever).
Oh the ideal moth should not be beautiful?
But accomplished, and magical too,
Plus he lived out of season,
Or in a year when it rained too much.
Sod off, I said, you make me cry
Please don't die.

DENIM HOAXTER

A jutted hip
A thumb stuck out
Rock 'n roll steps in Dr. Martens
Sex and innocence mixed
To the right degree
Casual, non-chalant
Yet wiser than the rest
A 24 hour creature
Who, yet, can be found mostly in bed
Planning the next sortie.

DESPERADOES

We searched for an answer for many years
But the question ran away from us
Sitting on the brink of the ultimate
Last boundary
Of the dreams we loved as children
We saw them shattered
And had to live on adrenaline
So we asked the question again and again
Until we got an answer.

DID YOU

Did you tune your guitar
Before you walked into the far
Distance
That separates your longing
From the place you want to get to?

Did you aim straight
As you shot your mouth off
Trying to say
What you thought today
In words everybody could understand?

Did you lie low
Listen to neither friend nor foe
As you made your decision
Of who you are
And who you'd like to be?

Did you listen well
When you heard of the hell
Some went through
Trying to get
Where you are bound?

Did you end your song
Trying to right the wrong
That you saw made
By something you can't evade
If you love life?

DREAMER

You wait and wait
For the fruits of your imagination
And while the day is long
There is no song
That can match your destination:
The land of dreams
Where everything is possible
No price is paid
And even love is admissible.

GAINING PERSPECTIVE

Telescope away from yourself
Into the stratosphere
The world as seen from a satellite
Look beneath your feet
Picture the fiery centre below
Cooling ever so slowly
Remember the tiny specks we seem to be
Between molten rock
And imponderable infinity
Even the most annoying word
And unthinkable nonsense
Then pales to an unseen ripple!

GRAND PRIX

The machines are designed
Ready to go
The contracts are signed
The crowd comes to the show
Skill, precision and a bit of God's luck
Drive to the limit, make the racing line
Speed is the essence
Careers wax and decline
And the champagne spouts
To mark the years going by.

To Ayrton Senna

Poetry from My Heart

GRIEF

Don't cry
The misery
Why?
Feel the strength
Of our love
Feel the strength
Of God's love
Feel the strength
Of the wind
Go down the road
To nowhere
With me
You'll end up somewhere
Where you're meant to be.

HAPPINESS

There must have been the first man to draw
The first man to speak
The first man to write
I'd like to be
The first to be perfectly happy
But I'm too late.

HAZY HOUR

I reached out and grabbed the magic potion
Ten ounces of devotion
A dram of love of life
A slice of hope to add the zest
But as I drank the hypnotizing
Sup of wishful thinking
Turned my bliss into doubt.

Welcome, you made it to the hazy hour
The hour where nothing's certain
But your positivity
Against the odds stacked by yourself
And everyone else
You've won
A flower smelling of love.

HORNY TOADS

inspired by "Time ain't nothing"

Walking into the sun
Down a dusty road
Leaving behind the bad stuff
Chewin' a piece of grass
Don't know what comes next
More of the bad, more of the good
Still your heart burns
'Cos life's worth the troubles
When the earth smells warm.

CERTAINITY

Long shadows loom
I feel smallish.
But friend,
I still feel alright
'Cos I know that the things I know
Cast equally long shadows of light.

HOUSEBOUND

Sitting on the windowsill
Watching the moon sitting still
I don't know what tomorrow will bring
Or what yesterday's song will sing
But the radio's churning out
Hits such as 'Twist and shout'
And I know I'm sitting in time
Somewhere without reason or rhyme
I can't be bothered to think
Anything but eternity and the kitchen sink.

ILLUSIONS

We think we got it so good it can't get better
We think we got it so bad it can't get worse
But babe, it's all an illusion
The reality is beyond your scope or mine
We can't understand
We're only a mite
Of the grand design done by someone with foresight
He wants us to push
To break out of the walls of common thought
For the answers become questions
When we're finally caught
In the ultimate illusion.

INDIGENOUS

I am part of the earth
And the earth is part of me
I can touch the stars with my soul
And maybe one day with my hand too
Nature is what keeps us alive.

INSIDE

Dancing in the ember twilight of the forest
The ghosts of your former selves
Drowning in the pools of the stew ponds
Your earlier fears and sorrows
Leaping over the clouds of Mars
Your hopes and joys magnified
Words cannot express
What you've got inside.

JUST LIKE THE INDIANS

We sat in a circle
A conspiracy
We pricked our thumbs
Let our blood mingle
Blood brothers were we.

Since those childhood days
I don't know the whereabouts
Of a single one of you
But I hope you carry the flag
Of freedom and friendship with you.

LEFT BEHIND

Jah said: If you changed your attitude
You might be getting somewhere
I gave you the ability for reproduction
You put it on a fleshy pedestal and groaned to it
Multiplying to the point of the absurd
I gave you fresh food to eat
You killed animals and roasted them
Gobbling their sizzling fat while you schemed
On how to divide and own
The earth that I gave you for free
I gave you the ability to invent
You made weapons to maim and destroy
And used them on each other
I gave you the ideas to get better
You turned them to religions
And killed each other over them
Now I'll just leave you to it
Until you catch up with me.

LEGACY OF DAMNATION

Walking down the road at night
I see the clusters
Of kids on the beer
Shouting abuse as they get near
The sky is blue
The moon is out
Their world is crumbling round about.

Reading the paper in the morning
Just as the sun is dawning
I see more tits and bums
Than real news
The degradation of sex
Into merchandise of scandal
Makes me wanting and turn into a vandal.

Going past a school
I see the children playing
What do we pass on to them
There is a saying
What you give is what you get
Do we pass on a rotten world
Is the collective heart really so cold?

LIFE'S EVERLASTING REVOLUTION

I lifted the lid off this Pandora's box
Found corpses of men rotting inside
Corpses of men less fortunate than me
Killed and maimed by the insanity
Of ways and teachings of the wrong way to be
I closed the lid and cried
At so much anguish and despair
Still the power that made us knew them as whole
And redeemed them
Like so many bottles at a candy store
It had the power to make the flowers bloom
The miser smile
To lift the curtain of doom
So the children of life's everlasting revolution
Would find home at the end of the day.

LONGING

Lady washing her coloured clothes by the river
She knows the song of the water
Hears the rush of the wavelets
Wishes.

Old man watching the passers by
On an empty road, wearing a battered hat
He knows his old age is nearly through
Contemplates.

Young boy watches them both from his bike
Knows his road is the same as theirs
Lives his days as full as he can
Dreams.

MAKING MONEY IN AN OFFICE

A weary trudge along set byways
The world might as well be a swamp
Impressions of interiors close up
Time takes on a wadded quality
A tick a buck
Who gives a ----
About the world outside of paper confines?

I do.

MISSISSIPPI SHACK

I was born in a Mississippi shack
I lost my virginity on the railroad track
I've got 6 children and they're all named Jack
Their father got lynched 'cos he was a doggone black
Been to Alaska and found my way back
Wrote for the Morning Star as a country hack
When I wrote the truth, I got the sack
I was born in a Mississippi shack
Where it stood they now sell crack
Made in a factory with a big chimney stack
Oh no, I'll never be going back
To that ole rat hole the Mississippi shack.

MOONLIGHT

The moon, our miniature satellite
Follows us around
Cool blue, icy pale or mellow 'n warm
Looks good,
Shines with the sun's reflected glow
Plays hide and seek
With the clouds, the earth 'n a plane or two
P'rhaps a satellite dish, a house or a hand
Smiles,
Is sometimes forgotten
At other times loved so
Is good for rhymes and stories –
Plus, have a laugh, it's always the same one.

OVER THE DUNE

The water's clear, the sun is right
The palm fronds shade
As you sip your heart's desire
But at what price?
Behind the dune the barbed wire coils
Like cattle treading in their own excrement
The other humanity, the dispossessed.

PEACE, BROTHER!

We planned the revolution
In every tiny detail
Like Arthur and his minions
In search of the Holy Grail
We planted bombs
We sang our songs
And many leaflets we did retail.
The revolution became a trend
We sold out easily
Someone a parcel did'st us send
We opened it dizzily
"Bomb the revolutionaries"
The speaking mechanism said
The semtex blew
The merchandise flew
And our leaders lost their heads.

PLEASED TO MEET YOU

I love the wind as it whistles thro' my hair
Do you?
I love positive vibes of any kind
Do you?
I love someone who'se upright and true
Do you?
I love to find sense in a muddled world
Do you?
I love to ask questions that dig up the truth
Do you?

PROTECTIVE

The fury of a torrent coming up against an outcrop
Smashing down in foaming splendour
Making a waterfall
On the edge of the world
Splashing the leaves
With the force of a steam train.

PSICHADELIA (Let the commonplace be fantastic)

Got lost this morning looking at the day
Unfolding and wanting me to play an act
As yet unwritten
Time runs ever forward
But for all we know
It may be backwards
To the sanity of wisdom
And peach blossom petals do exist
As do rainbows
Yet so often we walk around blindfolded
By our own ignorance
That an atom bomb could explode
And we'd only say
How does it affect me.
So watch the spider build his web
And realize it is a kitchen
With which you can decorate
The tip of a pencil.
(Spider permitting).

RAGAMUFFIN RAPPER

The ragamuffin beat
Of the man on the street
He pops his mouth out of joint
To make a hell of a point
He bops he beeps he bleeps
The audience captive keeps
Raps on about unity
How we should live with impunity
He tells us to make a choice
And listen to his boppy voice
The ragamuffin beat
Of the funny man on the street
Be Bop Shack Yeowl.

SELF THE HORSE

Twisting to an Irish jig
Riding a day and a night
And all life long
Hearsay has it that there is a lot wrong
With the human condition
But I am for the abolition of perdition
Takin' what ain't only yours
Is no one's at all
Sweat needs a reward
The horse needs a feed
And a cut will bleed.

SNOW HOUSE

Great gushing handfuls
Friable
Packed together it is elastic
It hurts when it hits you in the face
In a snow fight
Tracks you everywhere
And everywhere you leave tracks
Crystal water
Gives you cold feet
And a runny nose
If you want to be really cool
Build an igloo and live in it.

SOFTLY

Speak softly
A whisper of breath
Smile widely
Laugh with your heart.

SOLITARY GAMES

I wish I could have the winds at my command
So that they would blow the rain
Where it is needed
I wish politicians would listen more
To the warm earth demanding brotherhood
I wish for happiness for the lonely
That I was tall, so tall
I could study people's hairlines
And touch the stars
I wish for food for the hungry
The end of waste by affluence
And I wish I could play guitar so well
That it all came true
In six wistful chords.

STATURE

The wisdom of the trusting love
You forthrightly gave as a child
Comes back at you with the knowledge
Of other's feelings and your own worth
As you grow
You've begged and you've lorded
You've worried and boarded
You've scarpered and slung your hook
You've left behind the illusion
That you're greater than life
Or smaller than needed
You've come to the end of the road
And gone on
And now you know there's nothing to know
But the love that is strong
And the longing for home
And you.... ......

STATUS VICTIMS

The concept of status for most
Is based on power –
Buying
Military
Monetary
Sexual
Political
And more.
What is funny is
It smacks of insecurity.

SUPREMACY

Ma friend, de horse
He like to gallop free
He end up his days
Tethered in a stable.
Ma friend, de cow
She like to ruminate
She end up in the pan
Or just plain roasted in a bar-b-que.
Ma fried, de revolutionary
He like to live dreams
He ends up his days writing poetry
Which nobody reads 'cos he's boring.

TELLY

A cup of coffee
Brown sugar and cream
The perfect drink for a bit of media morphine
Meanwhile the coffee plantation worker
Sells his TV
To keep the wife and kids
In bread and tea
(Forms a co-operative
and buys a video recorder).

THE DRIPPING TAP

I crawled into a hole beneath
Lay curled up dreaming
Thinking all the while
What is my place in the universe
I asked advice from my surroundings
They told me that action
Is sometimes the easy way out
Learn how to contemplate
Said the dripping tap.
Stopped some days later at a service station
The gasoline drew heady fumes
From the depths of the earth
As the tap dripped danger
I realized the beauty
Of contemplation within action
And the motion of action
Within contemplation.

THE GLAMOUR OF VIOLENCE

Sitting watching Reservoir Dogs I thought
How many of us have had contact with violence
How many suffered it
How many wished it
How many watch it as if it was candy
Slashing at the pulse of our society
The irrational anger of the vein of hate –
Where does it come from?
We should be old enough to wait
Until the hate has passed
Find a solution that isn't quick and easy
And saves more than your own skin.

THE GREAT FILING CABINET IN THE SKY

Like dusty files in a large archive
Life's memories rest aligned
In our minds
Yet this vast trove of experiences
Are but a leaf
In the book of life on earth
Which is only a tome in the huge library
Of universal knowledge.
This library is so large
It takes a whole bunch of lifetimes
To just grasp a little of its essence
Which is why you get a ticket
With no expiry.

THE HAPPINESS MACHINE

It's got a face
Two arms
Eight little toes and two big ones
And is made in many models
How's yours doing?

THE LOVE THAT COMES FIRST

The baby
One day to be
An opinionated git
Looked at me
With loving eye
And said
Yes
Without speaking.

THE MAGICIAN'S APPRENTICE

The magician's apprentice
Climbed the year
To his ordainment
And slid down the other side
The squirrel that came up right close
Was amazed by his skills
But he thought: "There's always room
For improvement"
So he mixed his potions
For the hundredth time.

THE PAINT BOX

To some God is a light that blinds
To others it colours the world
To some the Great Spirit is as bland as a boiled egg
Others make him out as a salad with a bit of chili
To some there is no wisdom greater than a child's
Others think they themselves hold all the answers
To some there is no knowing how to limit
To others strictures are the be all and end all
Always we hold the paint box within ourselves
To draw what we perceive
The truth to us will always be
What we have outlined then to see.

THE SEAGULL

The seagull glides over our horizons
A messenger of nature
It catches our attention as it catches fish
A distraction from a focus
An attraction for rays of light
The song of the sea
Recedes into a murmur in the silence
Created by inner peace
Holding forth our being
To the past, present and future all at once
While the seagull glides.

THE SILVER BIRCHES

A van camped out with didgeridoo
The children played
The police joined in
The eco-warriors got tired
The law of exploitation won
The bulldozers moved in
Music got mournful
But the vegetation blooms on regardless.
We need our trees to live.
(The tree houses remain in our memories).

EPSOM '98

THE STATE OF THE UPPER LIMIT

A minimum income much above the poverty line
Guaranteed for one and all
A maximum income of comfortable wealth
Anything above that
Ploughed back into the general pool of resources
What do you think of that?

THE URCHIN

Hey, what's up
What's new with the world
Gawd, the air's sweet
Out here in the country
Where I can rest my city feet
I would like to be a big football star
Just like in my mama's melodramas
Grow old with my girlfriend
Play guitar and have friends at the bar
But now I suppose I should
Look for my next meal.

TRUE

Often to look out of someone else's eyes
You have to change your outlook
To something alien to yours
To see the beauty within
As well as the cobwebs and fire crackers
The disused rail tracks and stinging nettles
The pumpkins and the magic wand
That is what friendship makes worthwhile
At least when you're not at each other's throats
About invasion of privacy and all that
Or having a spat
About this or that
And old memories bring back others'
Cobwebs and firecrackers
Disused rail tracks and stinging nettles
Pumpkins
And the magic wand of life.

To Lenny Catterall

UNDER THE SUN

The sky is fiery red toning down to purple
The mesas and buttes absorb the heat
The sand stretches for miles like a fiery sea
Rippled by snake paths and fluted by the breeze
Which runs like hot breath over the hairs of your arms
As you sit contemplating majesty and infinity
And other worlds in which the cacti,
Rocks and dried out river beds
Are prominent features.

UNPREDICTABLE IMP

The secret of self hides in the deepest darkness
Half a lifetime and sometimes more
Is spent knocking at its door
But there's no answer
'Cos life's a man made web
Made of stuff built to avoid
This precious little mite
Which you keep hidden
The impish flame that only burns bright
When fed with truth and love
Stuff which this life needs
But our egos run from
Leaving the darkness to cover with weeds.

WAYWARD BLUES

You've been preaching at me for some time now
Well, all I can say
Is that I'll have to do the opposite now
To satisfy the rebel in me.

I may lose out, I may win
But I care as much
As a banana skin in the bin
Whether you're right or wrong.

I will laugh myself into some venture
That will kill the blues stone dead
Only for a moment in time
But what's eternity for anyway.....

Anyway.

WELL?

The gander's got a bump on his head
The bull's got pretty horns
The stag's proud of his antlers
But what does man have
That's worth the trouble?

WISE TEACHINGS

Hanging between a comma and a full stop
A single thought
The young you remembers it
But the words are naught
Like a caress in the back of the mind
Some stability it has wrought
But ask yourself what it is
And in indecision you are caught
Which means the thought is true.

X@4D.T.

I'd like to shoot the stars from the sky for you
Make flowers blossom for you
Clean up the world and see all the children smile
I'd walk a billion miles and a foot
Just to see you again.

ANGEL

I see you when I close my eyes
As real as my hand
Your dwelling is the deeper skies
I hope you've got a band
And play songs to the others
Who wait for us to find you
The living and dead have a bond
The mission is to overcome
Death of the soul

EVERY WAY

Sunshine, sunshine
You don't know what you're doing to me
Your absence is like a sore and chafed knee
Keeps reminding me of the summers gone
When I held your hand in a huff
'Cos we never had enough
But the sunflowers still grew
And every morning there was something new
In your play and smile
Life was growing for you mile by mile
The mystery we have in life
Was no reason for strife
I wish you well in your new days
But I miss you still in every way.